FLOWERS OF JAPAN

I0418851

First published in English in the United States of America in 2026 by
Rizzoli Electa, a Division of
Rizzoli International Publications, Inc.
49 West 27th Street
New York, NY 10001
rizzoliusa.com

Originally published in French in 2019 as
Les fleurs par les grands maîtres de l'estampe japonaise by
Éditions Hazan, an imprint of Hachette Livre, Vanves, France
editions-hazan.fr

For Rizzoli Electa
Publisher: Charles Miers
Associate Publisher: Margaret Rennolds Chace
Editor: Klaus Kirschbaum
Assistant Editor: Emily Ligniti
Translator: Liza Tripp

ISBN: 978-0-8478-7627-3
Library of Congress Control Number: 2025942944

Printed in China
2026 2027 2028 / 10 9 8 7 6 5 4 3 2 1

The authorized representative in the EU for product safety and compliance
is Mondadori Libri S.p.A., via Gian Battista Vico 42, Milan, Italy, 20123
mondadori.it

Visit us online
Facebook.com/RizzoliNewYork
Instagram.com/RizzoliBooks
Youtube.com/user/RizzoliNY

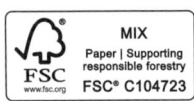

FLOWERS OF JAPAN
GREAT WORKS OF JAPANESE WOODBLOCK PRINTING

AMÉLIE BALCOU

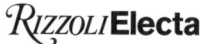

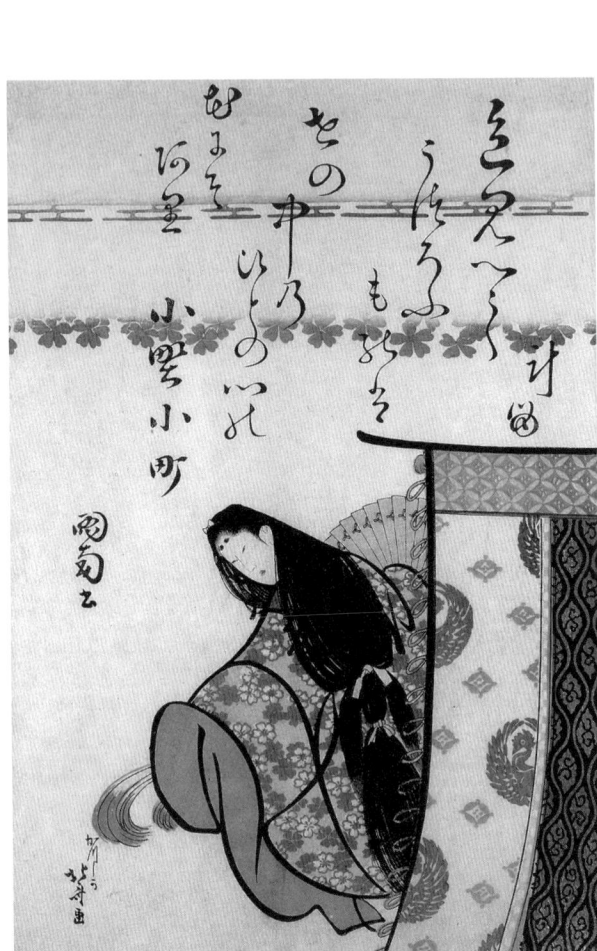

"Hokusai victoriously stripped his country's painting of Persian and Chinese influences and, through a study that was practically religious in nature, made it young again, reinvented it, and made it truly and fully Japanese. This universal painter brought the whole of his country's humanity into his work, reproducing man, woman, bird, fish, tree, flower, a blade of grass…with the liveliest drawings," exclaimed Edmond de Goncourt at the beginning of *Hokusaï*, published in 1896.[1]

A devoted Buddhist and animist, Katsushika Hokusai (1760–1849) explored the theme of nature extensively throughout his career. He began trying his hand at landscapes in the late eighteenth century, when he was still known as Shunrō. During this period, he apprenticed under the founder of the Katsukawa school, Katsukawa Shunshō, who was famous for his prints of actors. Hokusai was already experimenting with one-point perspective at this time, influenced by the West.

Around 1794, he became associated with the prestigious Tawaraya school, founded by Tawaraya Sōtatsu (who died in Kyoto around 1643), a great master of the Rinpa style of painting, which featured scenes exalting nature. Hokusai turned toward the art world of Kyoto, the capital and location of the emperor's court, which was largely affected by Chinese art. His contact with refined literary circles of poetry connoisseurs led him to develop a powerful lyrical style.[2] There was no doubt that during this period he learned to contemplate his environment in the manner of the ancient poets, who constantly celebrated nature, detailing its colors and behavior, impassioned by its tiniest variations, all considered ideal for delicate reveries. These poets did not describe nature but dreamed of it, fantasized about it, and imagined it so that each element became the bearer of a specific symbolic system.[3]

"The flowers' color/has withered, alas!/all the while, the gaze now lost/I think of my days escaping/into the night's unceasing rain,"[4] lamented the beautiful ninth-century poet Ono no Komachi (who Hokusai so loved to depict [p. 4]), contrasting flowers, an allegory of the ephemeral and brevity, with the sadness and obscurity of a gloomy rainy night, symbolizing a tragic outcome. Poets during the Heian period (794–1185), much influenced by the Chinese model, looked to nature to express their emotions, turning their attention toward the "sensitive world."

For Ki no Tsurayuki, who wrote the preface to *Kokin wakashū*, an anthology of waka poems, each comprised of five lines and thirty-one syllables, commissioned by Emperor Daigo in 905, "the poetry of the Yamato [Japanese] is rooted in the human heart and in pages of thousands of words. In this world, where men are subject to the most cumbersome occupations, poetry allows people to express what's in their hearts through what they see and hear. It's in flowers, in the song of a nightingale; in water, in the voice of a frog; upon hearing them, is he who lives without singing their song alive? That's what our poetry is—it's what moves sky and earth, rouses the pity of the invisible gods and demons, pours sweetness into man's ties to woman, and distracts the heart from ferocious warriors."[5]

This utopian, almost "codified" vision of nature had considerable influence on literature as well as art, notably the Kanō and Rinpa schools of painting. It should thus come as no surprise that Hokusai demonstrated such sensitivity to his environment.

Starting in the early nineteenth century, he adopted the ancient theme of *kachō-ga* (images of birds and flowers). This Chinese-inspired genre was fundamentally associated with the tradition of men of letters during the Heian period. Ubiquitous in painting since that time, it became an important element in printing by the late seventeenth century, first as a decorative feature on screens, partitions, and clothing, in particular in portraits of women (*bijin-ga*) or in erotic scenes—those "images of spring"—and later as an entirely separate theme in printed books.

Chinese flower albums—such as *Shi zhu zhai shu hua pu*, printed by Hu Zhengyan in 1643, or *Jieziyuan huazhuan*, published in China around 1679 to 1701, both reprinted in Japan in the 1750s—circulated widely in the archipelago. Hishikawa Moronobu (1618–1694), the first major representative of ukiyo-e, drew inspiration from them in several of his works dedicated to flowers and animals, such as *Kachō e-zukushi* in 1683. The genre expanded in the mid-eighteenth century. In 1746, Ōoka Shunboku (1680–1763), inspired by the paintings of the Ming dynasty (1368–1644) and notably by *Jieziyuan huazhuan*, published *Minchō seidō gaen*. It became a major theme of the Shijō school of painting, founded by Maruyama Ōkyo (1733–1795) and his former student Matsumura Goshun (1752–1811) in the late eighteenth century, and led to the publication of many picture albums (*gafu*).

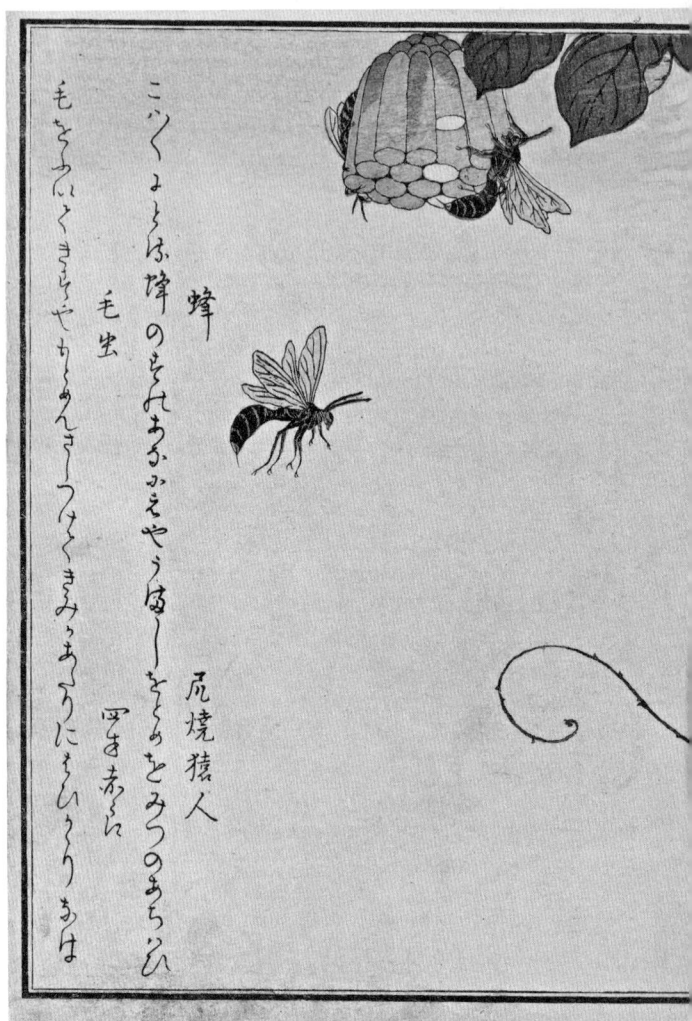

蜂

毛虫

こゝくよきほ蜂のをれまふかえやうはしをちをとみつのあちに

尻焼猿人

もさふにくきもろやちめんきゝつくきみゝあうりにもひろりもは

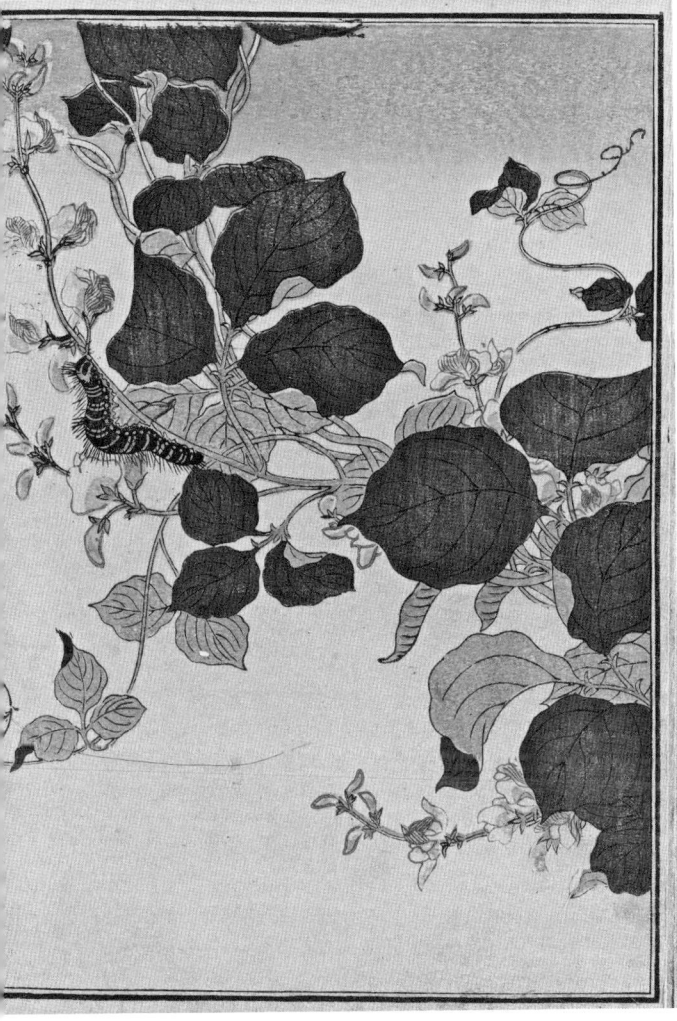

In the late eighteenth century, there were numerous artists devoted to *kachō-ga* prints or albums (often paired with poems), such as Kitao Shigemasa (1739–1820), Kitao Masayoshi (1764–1824), and Kitagawa Utamaro (circa 1753–1806). In 1789, Masayoshi created *Kaihaku raikin zui* (*Illustrated Catalog of Birds from Overseas*), while Utamaro published his famous *Ehon mushi erabi* (*Picture Book of Selected Insects* [pp. 8–9]) in 1788, followed by *Momo chidori kyōka-awase* (*Myriad Birds: Picture Book of Playful Verse*) around 1790.[6]

Starting in the early nineteenth century, this genre widely infused Hokusai's painting, in all likelihood influenced by Utamaro, Shigemasa, and Masayoshi but also by the Rinpa painter Sakai Hōitsu (1761–1829). He also created many *surimono*, which were prints adorned with poems. *Kachō-ga* nevertheless remained a secondary, mostly decorative element, and Hokusai was more concerned with landscapes.

After establishing his own studio in 1798, Hokusai particularly devoted himself to the art of illustration and image collection. He also published his first albums, which were notably comprised of famous views of Japan and already a testament to his significant confidence in the landscape genre, such as *Panoramic Views of Both Banks of the Sumida River at a Glance* (circa 1804) and *Fine Views of the Eastern Capital at a Glance* (circa 1800).[7] The illustration of *kyōka* poems and *yomihon* "books of readings," with their fanciful and extraordinary plots inspired by the legendary past and Chinese literature, were likewise ripe for experimentation with landscapes and nature.[8]

By 1810, Hokusai shifted to publishing didactic works (*edehon*), filled with thousands of sketches and models to copy, all demonstrating his graphic expertise. Between 1812 and

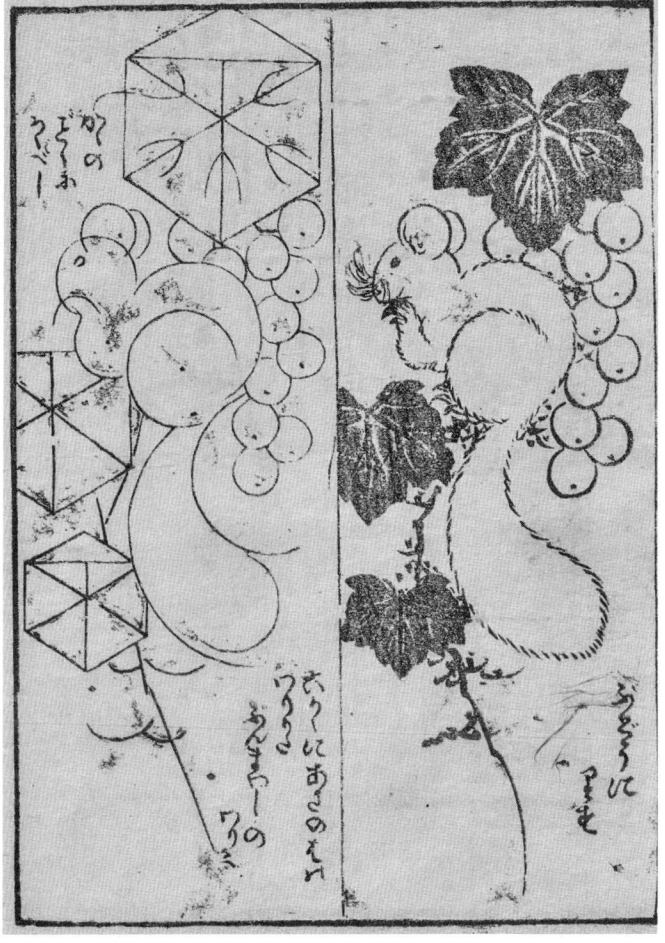

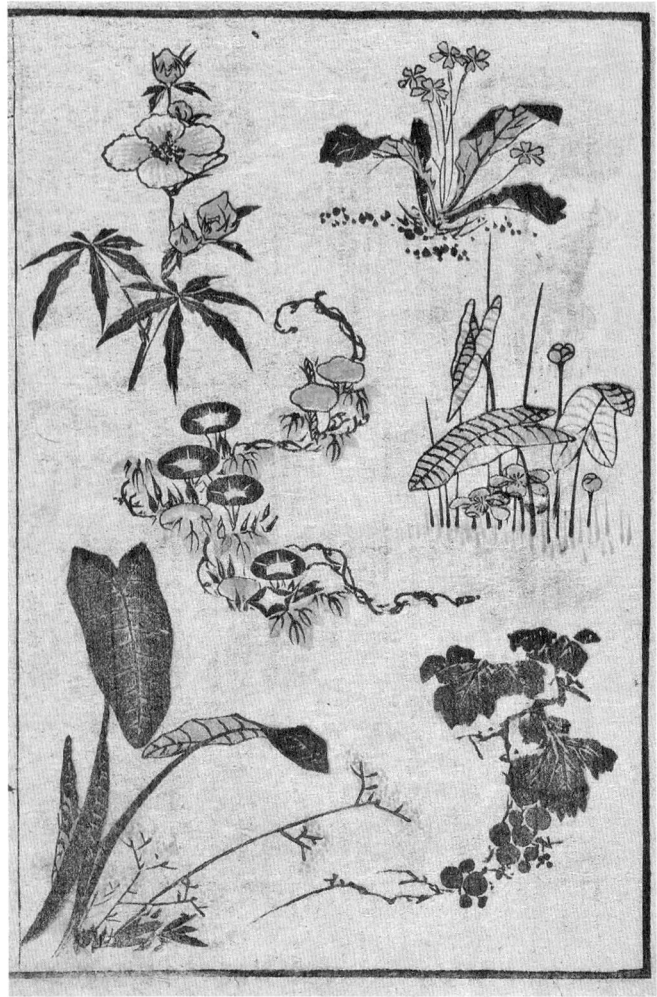

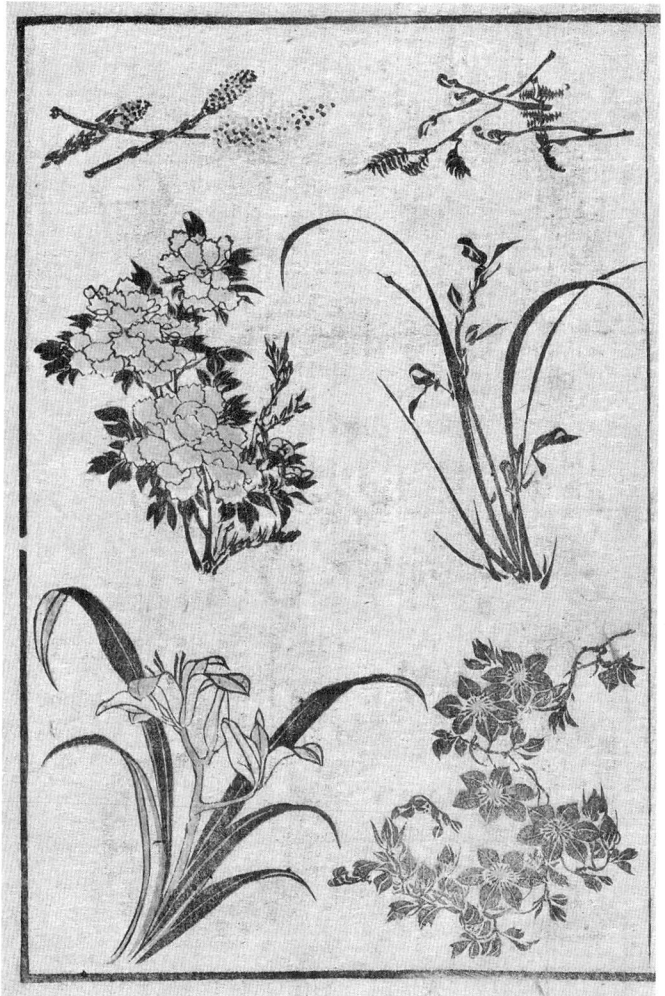

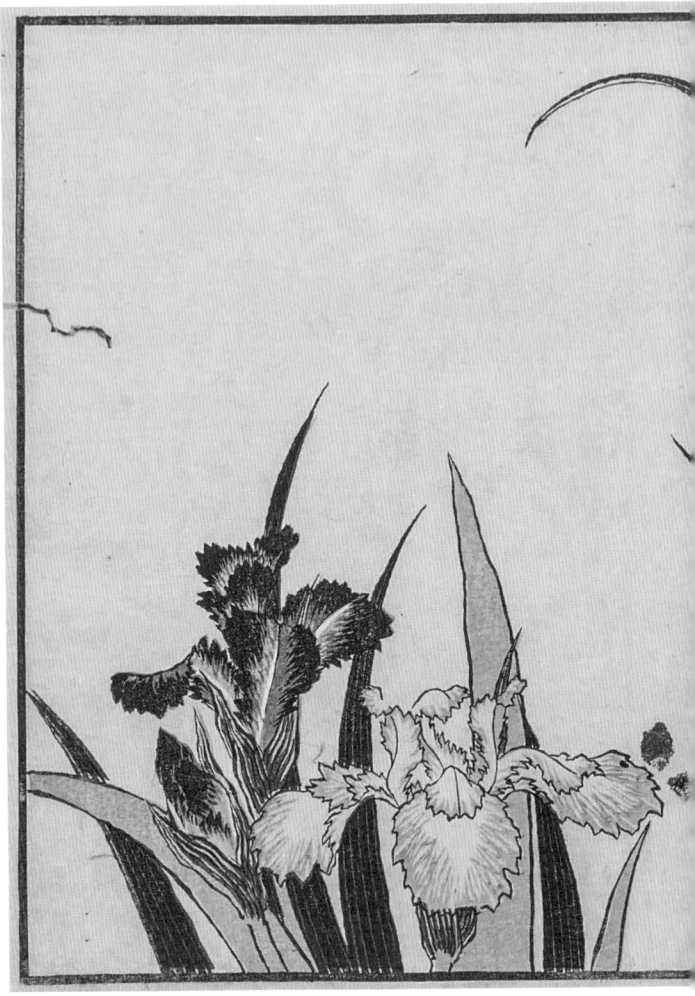

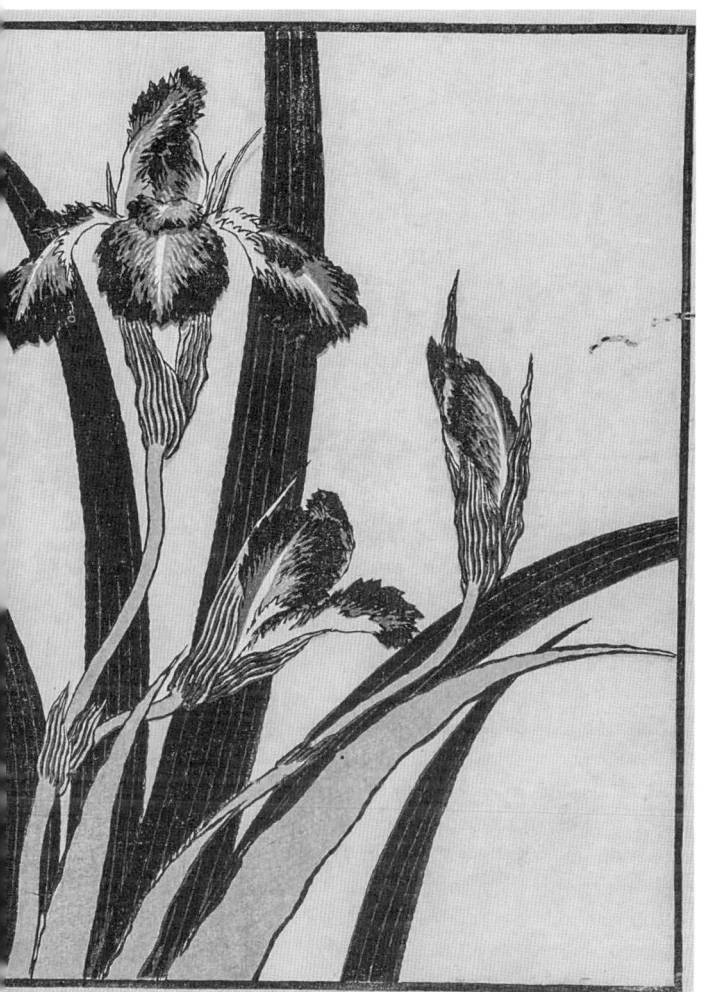

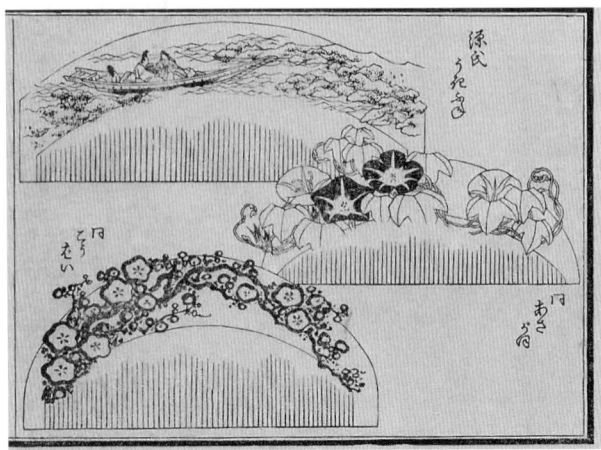

1814, he created two volumes of *Quick Lessons in Simplified Drawing* (p. 11), imparting the fundamentals of drawing with the help of a compass and ruler.[9] Hokusai's interest in this type of work was confirmed in 1814: he published the nature-inspired *Hokusai's Album of Pictures from Nature* (pp. 14–15), which heralded his later series on flowers, as well as the first volume of his behemoth *Manga* (pp. 12–13), which teemed with motifs in all genres connected to fauna, flora, landscapes, daily life, and even the supernatural.[10] The endeavor was an immediate success that would result in a collection of fifteen volumes, which were only published in their entirety in 1878 after Hokusai's death. The collection features an abundance of nature studies and sketches. This time, the theme was sufficient in and of itself, and the work showed nearly the same autonomy as his later flower series.

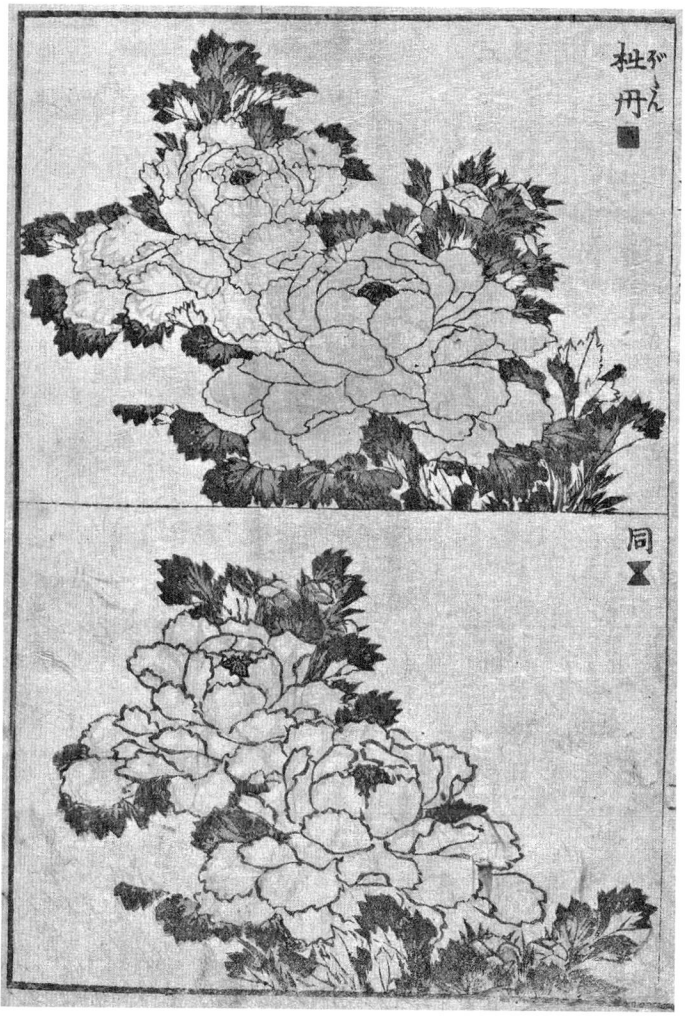

His virtuosic and complex *Three Styles of Drawing* (p. 17) published in 1816, which transposed a single subject into three different pictural styles, also abounds with naturalist motifs. Between 1817 and 1818, Hokusai drew both parts of *The Quick Pictorial Dictionary,* a veritable dictionary of pictorial motifs with 1,349 plates, before publishing the memorable *Picture Album of Drawings at One Stroke* in 1823.

Hokusai practiced his craft fiercely, letting loose, overcome by an absolute drawing frenzy, even composing several volumes for artisans, such as *Modern Designs for Combs and Pipes* (1822–23) (p. 16), *New Forms for Design* (1824) for the textile industry, and *Picture Book of New Designs for the Various Crafts* (1836). These numerous works attest to his unprecedented imagination and perception of volume, form, and color, which would again be expressed to beautiful effect in *Picture Book on the Use of Coloring* (p. 20), published in 1848, one year before his death.[11]

In the 1820s, a period when the middle class had begun taking interest in *surimono,* Hokusai provided, in addition to multiple *kachō-ga* paintings, lovely series on nature, such as *A Matching Game with Genroku-period Poem Shells* around 1821 (p. 19).

In the early 1830s, when the use of brighter and longer-lasting artificial pigments, like Prussian blue, revolutionized printmaking, Hokusai won recognition for his famous *Thirty-six Views of Mount Fuji*, which were sumptuously printed in large, wide format.[12] By publishing one of the first great series uniquely dedicated to landscapes, and using Prussian blue on a broad scale, he brought acclaim to the landscape genre and themes of nature, which, although

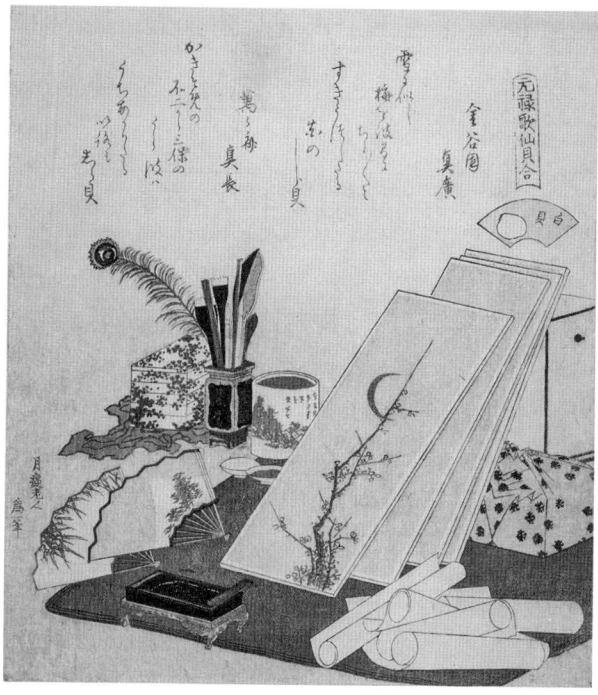

ubiquitous in painting, were at that time still undervalued by printmakers.[13]

Members of the Chōnin middle class, who were the primary consumers of prints, took an avid interest in the depictions of peasants and laborers working in front of Mount Fuji, fishermen sailing on the Sumida River, and travelers or merchants loaded with packages plodding up the mountain.

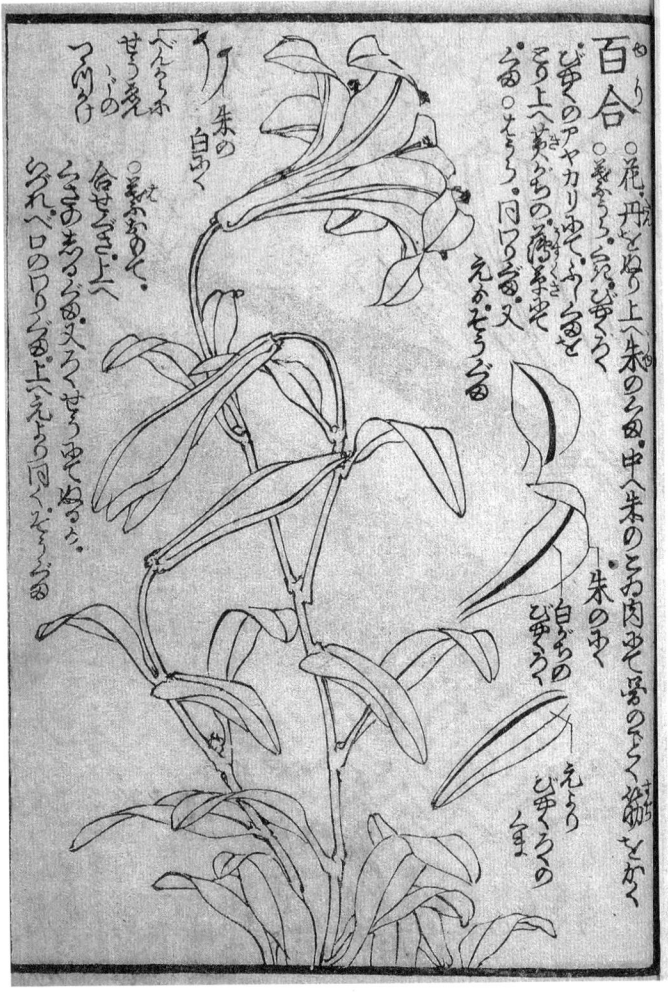

The Tokugawa shogunate, which had restricted travel in the country, was on the decline, and people could again move about freely and traverse the roads of Japan. Entirely absorbed in contemplating a rediscovered natural world, Hokusai went out in search of *meisho* (famous places), picturesque landscapes, spectacular waterfalls, exotic flowers, and dizzyingly high bridges, at a time when Japanese printmaking was just beginning to decline as a result of the conservative Tokugawa regime, which had increased its edicts throughout the Edo period. Japanese printmaking would moreover remain hindered by censorship from the Tenpō reforms introduced between 1841 and 1843, which notably once again limited the number of colors and restored the ban on depicting erotic scenes or those involving courtesans or actors.[14]

Hokusai rapidly completed *One Hundred Views of Mount Fuji* (1834) and published numerous sequels dedicated to *kachō-ga* or landscapes, such as *Eight Views of Ryūkyū* (1833) representing exotic and phantasmagoric views, *A Tour of Waterfalls in Various Provinces* (1833–34), and *Remarkable Views of Bridges in Various Provinces* (1834).

Between 1830 and 1832, he composed, in keeping with *Hokusai's Album of Pictures from Nature*, an untitled series of ten large-format horizontal prints, most often pairing animals with luxurious vegetation, like a grasshopper with irises (fig. 4) or a butterfly with peonies (fig. 1); it is now known as *Large Flowers* series, in contrast with the later *Small Flowers* series in a narrower format, published around 1834. While the pigments used were not as bright as those in *Small Flowers*, this was the first major series solely dedicated to *kachō-ga*, printed on plain paper, widthwise and in large format—nature, alone and sovereign.

Around 1832 to 1833, Hokusai drew a series of *Large Flower and Bird Prints*, pairing large birds, waders, and raptors with the various seasons of the year, before tackling *Small Flowers* around 1834, which he matched with Chinese or Japanese poems. This time, the use of brighter, longer-lasting artificial pigments truly revolutionized the genre, which reached its peak in prints with an abundance of colors, which until then had only been permitted in painting.

Small Flowers series would considerably influence the work of Utagawa Hiroshige (1797–1858), the great landscape master and an admirer of Hokusai, who shortly completed more than two hundred *kachō-ga* prints, many in vertical format and paired with poems that referred to the seasons.

Despite these influences, Hiroshige developed his own unique style. Hokusai studied and precisely and almost scientifically analyzed nature and its representations, no doubt affected by the West and by Dutch botanical treatises. Hiroshige broke things down, daring to simplify almost to the point of abstraction and proposing novel compositions. Such was the case with his bird viewed from below, perched on the branch of a morning glory invading the print (fig. 3), forming a composition to which Utagawa Hiroshige III would return around 1871 to 1873 (fig. 65). He innovatively paired landscape with *kachō-ga*, notably in *One Hundred Famous Views of Edo*, which contrasted a green foreground with a landscape view, and in *Horikiri Iris Gardens* (fig. 44) and *Plum Garden at Kameido*, which employed a type of composition that his student Utagawa Hiroshige II (Shigenobu) would frequently revisit.

By the nineteenth century, Hokusai and Hiroshige had extensively influenced artists like Keisai Eisen (1790–1848) and Utagawa Kuniyoshi (1797–1861), as well as impressionists in the West. While Japanese printing began to decline in the late nineteenth century, *kachō-ga* no less remained one of the main themes valued by the great representatives of the *shin-hanga* (new woodcut prints) movement, such as Imao Keinen (1845–1924) and Ohara Shōson (1877–1945), who breathed new life into printmaking techniques in the early twentieth century.

Later on, as numerous disasters led humans to question their relationships with nature, *kachō-ga* would remain a great source of inspiration for artists like Hiramatsu Reiji (born 1941), Tamako Kataoka (1905–2008), Togyū Okumura (1889–1990), and Atsushi Uemura (1933–2024), and even for animated films, as in the work of Hayao Miyazaki (born 1941), the director of *Princess Mononoke* (1997), *Spirited Away* (2001), and *Howl's Moving Castle* (2004).

[1] Edmond de Goncourt, *Hokusaï*. Paris: G. Charpentier et E. Fasquelle, 1896, pp. 1–2.

[2] Gian Carlo Calza, *Hokusai*. Paris: Phaidon, 2005, pp. 104–7.

[3] Claire-Akiko Brisset, "Peinture et saisons au Japon: une poétique du temps et du lieu," in Christine Shimizu (ed.), *Le Japon au fil des saisons: collection Robert et Betsy Feinberg*. Paris: Paris Musées, 2014, pp. 39–45. Exhibition catalog.

[4] Poem from *Recueil de poèmes de jadis et de naguère (Kokin wakashū)*, in *Anthologie de la poésie japonaise classique*, trans. Gaston Renondeau. Paris: Gallimard, 1971, p. 121.

[5] Georges Bonneau, *Le Monument poétique de Heian: Le Kokinshū*, vol. 1. Paris: Librairie orientaliste Paul Geuthner, 1933, pp. 27–9.

[6] Amy Reigle Newland (ed.), *The Hotei Encyclopedia of Japanese Woodblock Prints*. Amsterdam: Hotei Publishing, 2005, pp. 214–15.

[7] Matthi Forrer, *Hokusai. Coup d'œil sur les deux rives de la rivière Sumida suivi de la rivière Yôdo*. Paris: Hazan, 2012.

[8] Makoto Takemura, "Les livres imprimés," in *Hokusai*. Paris: Réunion des musées nationaux, 2014, pp. 52–6. Exhibition catalog.

[9] Manuela Moscatiello, *Hokusai. Manuels de dessin*, trans. Béatrice Robert-Boissier. Arles: Éditions Philippe Picquier, 2016, pp. 10–25.

[10] Takemura, Op. cit., pp. 52–6.

[11] Ibid., pp. 52–6.

[12] Sarah E. Thompson, "Censorship and Ukiyo-e prints," in Amy Reigle Newland (ed.), *The Hotei Encyclopedia*. Amsterdam: Hotei Publishing, 2005, pp. 214–15.

[13] Jocelyn Bouquillard, *Hokusai: Les Trente-six vues du mont Fuji*. Paris: Seuil, 2010, pp. 7–13; *Hokusai*, Exhibition catalog, p. 282.

[14] Thompson, Op. cit., pp. 214–15.

p. 4 | Katsushika Hokusai
The Poetess Ono no Komachi
series: *Six Immortal Poets*,
ca. 1810
oban size, 38 x 26 cm
Chicago, The Art Institute
of Chicago (1961.162)

pp. 8–9 | Kitagawa Utamaro
Picture Book of Selected Insects
publisher: Tsutaya Jūzaburō
(Koshodo), 1788
chuban size, 25 x 18 cm
Amsterdam, Rijksmuseum
(RP-P-1960-10B-3)

p. 11 | Katsushika Hokusai
Quick Lessons in Simplified Drawings, vol. 1
publisher: Tsutaya Jūzaburō
(Koshodo), 1812
hanshibon size, 18.4 x 13 cm
Boston, Museum of Fine Arts
(1997.895)

pp. 12–13 | Katsushika Hokusai
Manga, vol. 1
publishers: Eirakuya Toshiro (Nagoya),
Kadomaruya Jinsuke (Edo), 1814
chuban size, 22.7 x 15.8 cm
New York, The Metropolitan
Museum of Art (JIB111a)

pp. 14–15 | Katsushika Hokusai
Hokusai's Album of Pictures from Nature
1814
ohon size, 25.8 x 17.1 cm
Boston, Museum of Fine Arts
(1997.883)

p. 16 | Katsushika Hokusai
Modern Designs for Combs and Pipes
ca. 1822–23
hanshibon size, 18.3 x 13 cm
Boston, Museum of Fine Arts
(1997.885.1-3)

p. 17 | Katsushika Hokusai
Three Styles of Drawing
1816
chuban size, 22.5 x 15.6 cm
Washington, DC, Smithsonian
Libraries (39088018834994)

p. 19 | Katsushika Hokusai
*The Studio, Illustration for
The White Shell (Shiragai)*
series: *A Matching Game with
Genroku-period Poem Shells*,
ca. 1821
shikishiban size, 20.2 x 17.7 cm
Chicago, The Art Institute
of Chicago (1936.280)

p. 20 | Katsushika Hokusai
Picture Book on the Use of Coloring
1848
hanshibon size, 18.3 x 12.9 cm
New York, The Metropolitan
Museum of Art (2013.881)

1 | Katsushika Hokusai
Peonies and Butterfly
series: *Large Flowers,* publisher:
Nishimuraya Yohachi (Eijudo),
ca. 1833–34
oban size, 26.3 x 39 cm
Boston, Museum of Fine Arts
(11.17593)

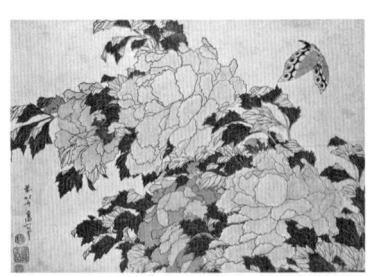

2 | Utagawa Hiroshige
Crested Yellow Bird and Hibiscus
ca. 1832
chu-tanzaku size, 37.8 x 13 cm
New York, The Metropolitan
Museum of Art (JP2485)

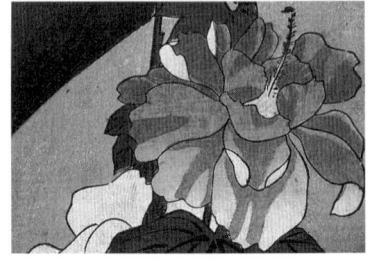

3 | Utagawa Hiroshige
Morning Glories and Bird
ca. 1840–50
ai-tanzaku size, 32.7 x 12.2 cm
New York, The Metropolitan
Museum of Art (JP1488)

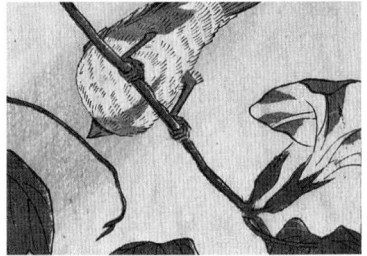

4 | Katsushika Hokusai
Grasshopper and Iris
series: *Large Flowers,* publisher:
Nishimuraya Yohachi (Eijudo),
ca. 1820s
oban size, 24.8 x 36 cm
New York, The Metropolitan
Museum of Art (JP747)

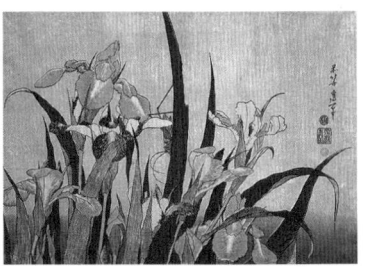

Ohara Shōson
Iris
publisher: Kawaguchi Jirō, ca. 1930
oban size, 32.1 x 21.4 cm
Minneapolis, Minneapolis
Institute of Art (P.75.51.189)
(detail, **see 74**)

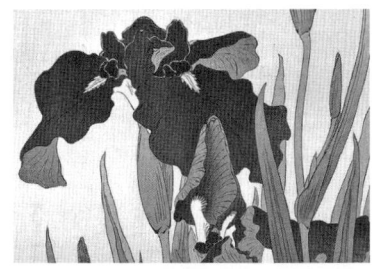

5 | Katsushika Hokusai
Bullfinch and Weeping Cherry
series: *Small Flowers*, publisher:
Nishimuraya Yohachi (Eijudo), ca. 1834
chuban size, 25.5 x 18.7 cm
Boston, Museum of Fine Arts
(21.10229)

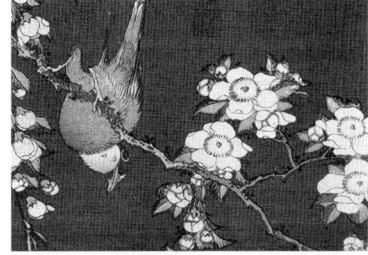

6 | Katsushika Hokusai
Peonies and Canary
series: *Small Flowers*, publisher:
Nishimuraya Yohachi (Eijudo),
ca. 1834
chuban size, 25.4 x 18.7 cm
Minneapolis, Minneapolis
Institute of Art (74.1.205)

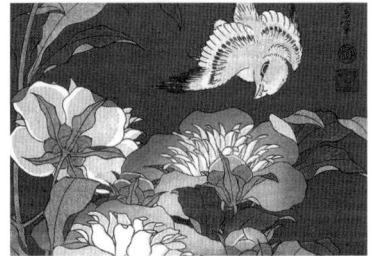

7 | Katsushika Hokusai
Morning Glories and Tree Frog
series: *Large Flowers*, publisher:
Nishimuraya Yohachi (Eijudo),
ca. 1833–34
oban size, 26.7 x 39 cm
Boston, Museum of Fine Arts (06.1307)

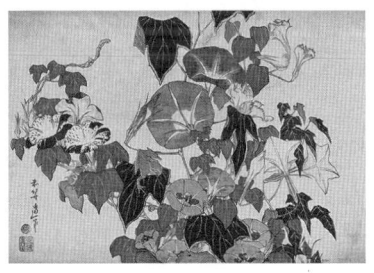

8 | Utagawa Hiroshige
Camellia and Finch
ca. 1840
ai-tanzaku size, 33 x 10.8 cm
New York, The Metropolitan
Museum of Art (JP258)

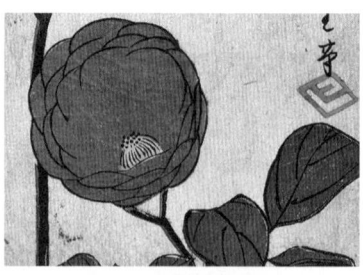

9 | Utagawa Hiroshige
Morning Glories
ca. 1843
ai-tanzaku size, 32.9 x 11.1 cm
New York, The Metropolitan
Museum of Art (JP265)

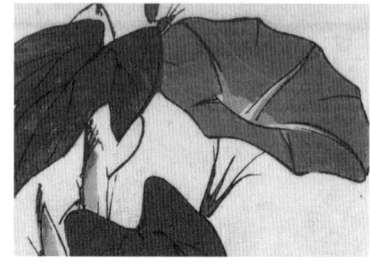

10 | Utagawa Hiroshige
Grasshopper and Morning-Glory Vine
publisher: Kawaguchiya Shōzō
(Shoeido, Eisendo), ca. 1835
chu-tanzaku size, 36.2 x 12.7 cm
New York, The Metropolitan
Museum of Art (JP2533)

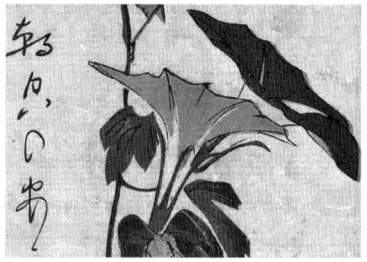

11 | Utagawa Hiroshige
Blue Bird
publisher: Kawaguchiya Shōzō
(Shoeido, Eisendo), ca. 1830
chu-tanzaku size, 37.1 x 12.7 cm
New York, The Metropolitan
Museum of Art (JP3147)

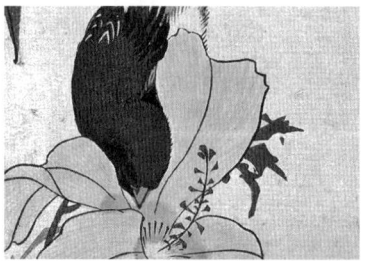

12 | Utagawa Hiroshige
A Peacock Perched on a Maple Tree
ca. 1833
chu-tanzaku size, 37.6 x 12.7 cm
New York, The Metropolitan
Museum of Art (JP269)

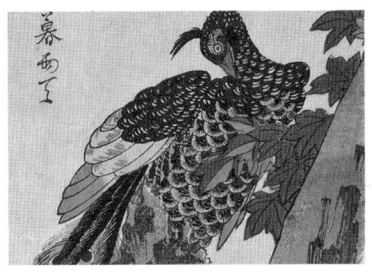

13 | Utagawa Hiroshige
Eastern Grey Wagtail and Rose
ca. 1830
ai-tanzaku size, 34.3 x 11.4 cm
New York, The Metropolitan
Museum of Art (JP238)

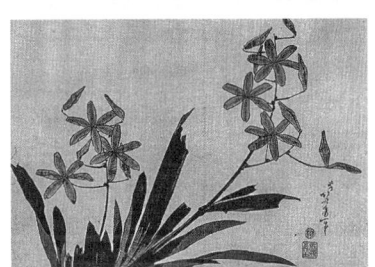

14 | Katsushika Hokusai
Blackberry Lily
series: *Large Flowers*, publisher:
Nishimuraya Yohachi (Eijudo),
ca. 1833–34
oban size, 26.2 x 38.5 cm
Boston, Museum of Fine Arts
(11.17597)

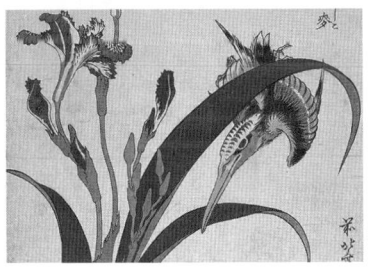

15 | Katsushika Hokusai
Kingfisher with Iris and Wild Pinks
series: *Small Flowers*, publisher:
Nishimuraya Yohachi (Eijudo), ca. 1834
chuban size, 25.8 x 18.7 cm
Boston, Museum of Fine Arts
(21.10221)

16| Katsushika Hokusai
Hawfinch and Marvel-of-Peru
series: *Small Flowers,* publisher:
Nishimuraya Yohachi (Eijudo), ca. 1834
chuban size, 25.7 x 18.5 cm
Boston, Museum of Fine Arts
(11.20437)

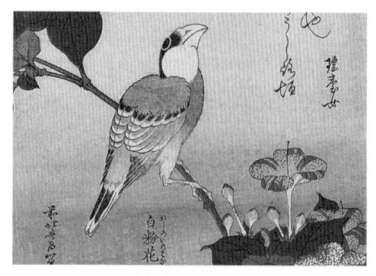

17| Katsushika Hokusai
Lilies
series: *Large Flowers,* publisher:
Nishimuraya Yohachi (Eijudo),
ca. 1833–34
oban size, 24.9 x 36.1 cm
Minneapolis, Minneapolis
Institute of Art (74.1.214)

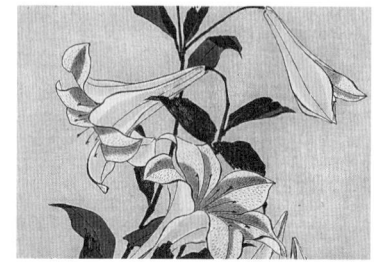

Ohara Shōson
White Lilies
publisher: Kawaguchi, ca. 1930
oban size, 32.5 x 22 cm
Amsterdam, Rijksmuseum
(RP-P-1999-542)
(detail, **see 69**)

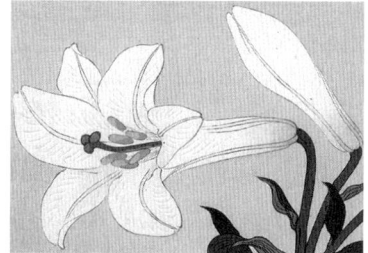

18| Katsushika Hokusai
Hydrangeas and Swallow
series: *Large Flowers,* publisher:
Nishimuraya Yohachi (Eijudo),
ca. 1833–34
oban size, 26.2 x 38.1 cm
Boston, Museum of Fine Arts
(11.17592)

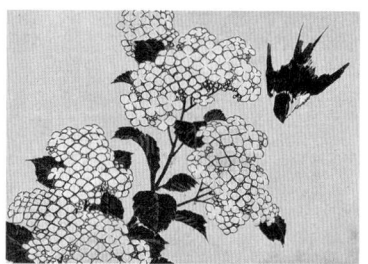

19 | Katsushika Hokusai
Dragonfly and Bellflower
series: *Large Flowers*, publisher:
Nishimuraya Yohachi (Eijudo),
ca. 1833–34
oban size, 26.7 x 38.1 cm
Amsterdam, Rijksmuseum
(RP-P-1988-349)

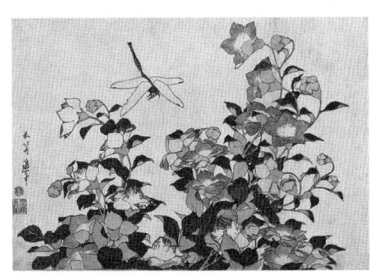

20 | Katsushika Hokusai
Java Sparrow on Magnolia
series: *Small Flowers*, publisher:
Nishimuraya Yohachi (Eijudo), ca. 1834
chuban size, 25.6 x 18.6 cm
Boston, Museum of Fine Arts
(11.20436)

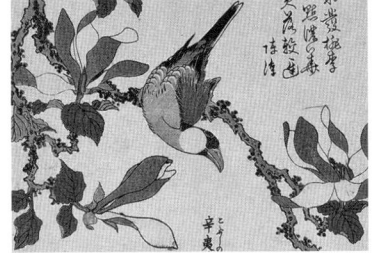

21 | Katsushika Hokusai
Wagtail and Wisteria
series: *Small Flowers*, publisher:
Nishimuraya Yohachi (Eijudo), ca. 1834
chuban size, 24.8 x 18.2 cm
Washington, DC, National Museum
of Asian Art (S2004.3.213)

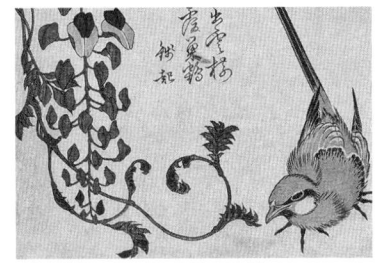

22 | Tanigami Konan
Cyclamen
ca. 1910
Private Collection

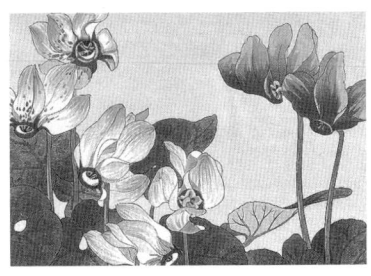

23 | Utagawa Hiroshige
Red Blossom Plum
ca. 1847
chu-tanzaku size, 34.6 x 11.4 cm
New York, The Metropolitan
Museum of Art (JP2527)

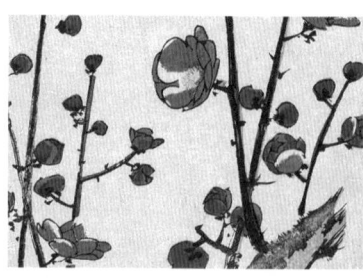

24 | Utagawa Hiroshige
Long-Tailed Tit on Autumn Ivy
ca. 1835
chu-tanzaku size, 37.5 x 12.1 cm
New York, The Metropolitan
Museum of Art (JP2536)

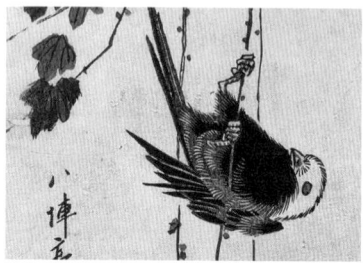

25 | Utagawa Hiroshige
Hibiscus Mutabilis and Long-Tailed Bird
publisher: Kawaguchiya Shōzō
(Shoeido, Eisendo), ca. 1842
ai-tanzaku size, 33.2 x 11.4 cm
New York, The Metropolitan
Museum of Art (JP263)

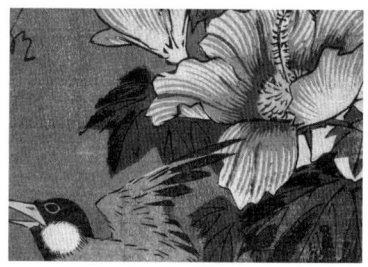

26 | Utagawa Hiroshige
Bird and Iris
ca. 1840
ai-tanzaku size, 33.2 x 11 cm
New York, The Metropolitan
Museum of Art (JP1897)

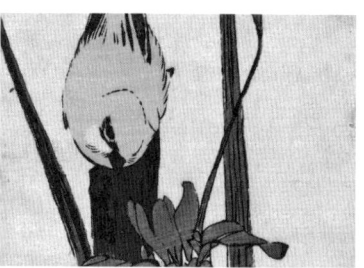

27 | Katsushika Hokusai
Hibiscus and Sparrow
series: *Large Flowers*, publisher:
Nishimuraya Yohachi (Eijudo),
ca. 1833–34
oban size, 24.9 x 36.3 cm
Minneapolis, Minneapolis
Institute of Art (74.1.213)

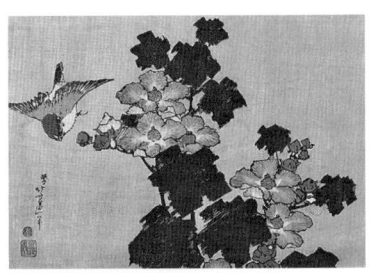

28 | Katsushika Hokusai
Shrike and Blessed Thistle
series: *Small Flowers*, publisher:
Nishimuraya Yohachi (Eijudo), ca. 1834
chuban size, 25.5 x 18.8 cm
Boston, Museum of Fine Arts
(21.10226)

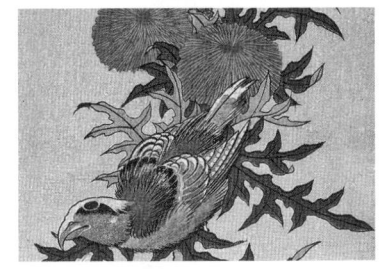

29 | Katsushika Hokusai
*Shrike and Bluebird with Begonia
and Wild Strawberry*
series: *Small Flowers*, publisher:
Nishimuraya Yohachi (Eijudo), ca. 1834
chuban size, 25.5 x 15.4 cm
Boston, Museum of Fine Arts
(11.20455)

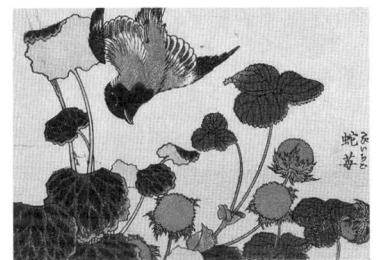

30 | Katsushika Hokusai
Warbler and Roses
series: *Small Flowers*, publisher:
Nishimuraya Yohachi (Eijudo), ca. 1834
chuban size, 25.7 x 18.5 cm
Boston, Museum of Fine Arts
(11.17616)

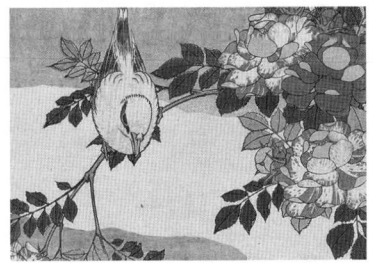

31 | Katsushika Hokusai
Cuckoo and Azaleas
series: *Small Flowers*, publisher:
Nishimuraya Yohachi (Eijudo), ca. 1834
chuban size, 24.1 x 19 cm
Boston, Museum of Fine Arts
(11.23023)

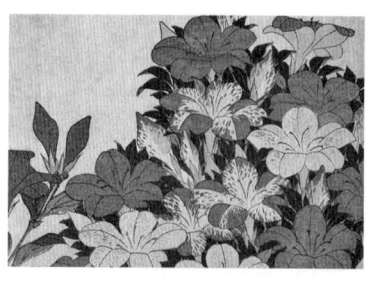

32 | Katsushika Hokusai
Chrysanthemums and Horsefly
series: *Large Flowers*, publisher:
Nishimuraya Yohachi (Eijudo),
ca. 1833–34
oban size, 24.6 x 36.7 cm
Minneapolis, Minneapolis
Institute of Art (74.1.210)

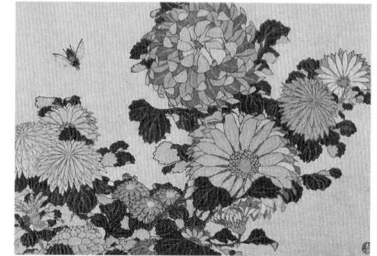

33 | Utagawa Hiroshige
Rose
ca. 1843–47
ai-tanzaku size, 33.3 x 11 cm
New York, The Metropolitan
Museum of Art (JP3151)

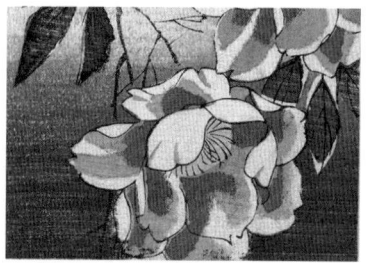

34 | Utagawa Hiroshige
Peony and Cock
1854
ai-tanzaku size, 33.3 x 11.1 cm
New York, The Metropolitan
Museum of Art (JP2526)

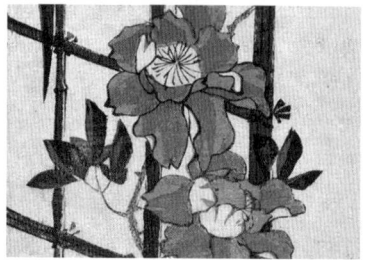

35 | Katsushika Hokusai
Poppies
series: *Large Flowers*, publisher:
Nishimuraya Yohachi (Eijudo),
ca. 1833–34
oban size, 26.2 x 38.4 cm
Boston, Museum of Fine Arts
(11.17594)

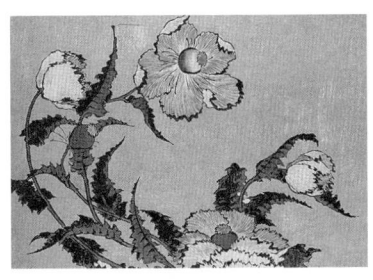

36 | Utagawa Hiroshige
Pear Blossoms and Swallows
ca. 1840
ai-tanzaku size, 33.3 x 11.1 cm
New York, The Metropolitan
Museum of Art (JP262)

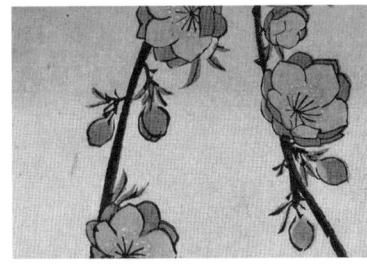

37 | Utagawa Hiroshige
Sparrow and Hibiscus
publisher: Sanoya Kihei (Kikakudo),
ca. 1834
chu-tanzaku size, 34.3 x 11.4 cm
New York, The Metropolitan
Museum of Art (JP2462)

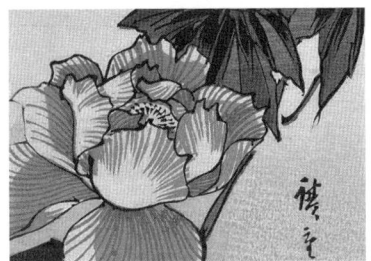

38 | Utagawa Hiroshige
A Pair of Quails and Poppies
publisher: Kawaguchiya Shōzō
(Shoeido, Eisendo), ca. 1835
chu-tanzaku size, 35.6 x 12.7 cm
New York, The Metropolitan
Museum of Art (JP239)

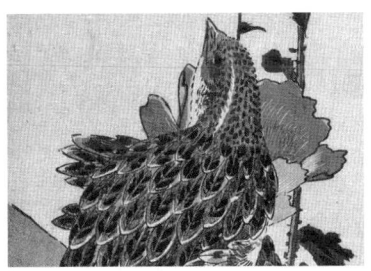

39 | Utagawa Hiroshige
Eastern Grey Wagtail and Rose
ca. 1830
ai-tanzaku size, 34.3 x 11.4 cm
New York, The Metropolitan
Museum of Art (JP238)

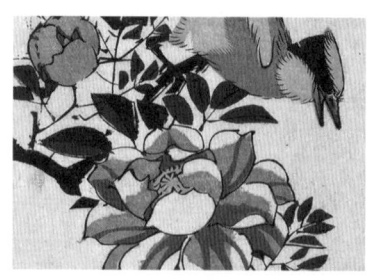

40 | Utagawa Hiroshige
*Japanese White-Eye and Titmouse
on a Camellia Branch*
publisher: Maruya Seijiro
(Maursei, Jukakudo), ca. 1840
chuban size, 26 x 18.4 cm
New York, The Metropolitan
Museum of Art (JP250)

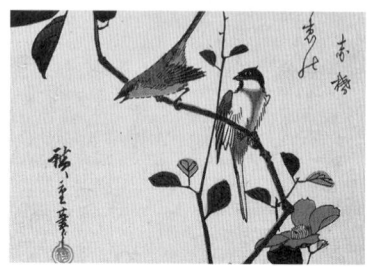

41 | Utagawa Hiroshige
Swallows and Kingfisher with Rose Mallows
publisher: Maruya Seijiro (Marusei,
Jukkakudo), ca. 1838
chuban size, 26.5 x 18.7 cm
New York, The Metropolitan
Museum of Art (JP249)

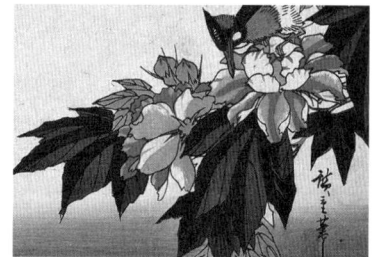

Ohara Shōson
Great Tit on Paulownia Branch
publisher: Watanabe Shōzaburō,
ca. 1925–36
oban size, 38.1 x 25.9 cm
Amsterdam, Rijksmuseum
(RP-P-1999-375)
(detail, **see 78**)

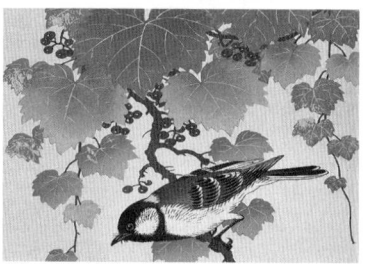

42 | Utagawa Hiroshige
Swallow and Wisteria
ca. 1840
chuban size, 22.5 x 16.8 cm
New York, The Metropolitan
Museum of Art (JP254)

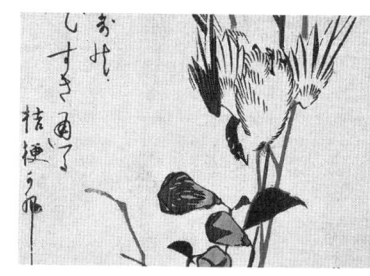

43 | Utagawa Hiroshige
Large-Flowered Flat Bill and Sparrow
ca. 1833
chuban size, 22.7 x 17 cm
New York, The Metropolitan
Museum of Art (JP251)

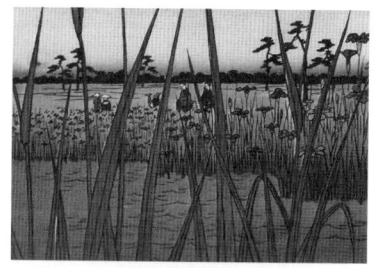

44 | Utagawa Hiroshige
Horikiri Iris Garden
series: *One Hundred
Famous Views of Edo*, 1857
oban size, 37 x 24.9 cm
Amsterdam, Rijksmuseum
(RP-P-1968-17)

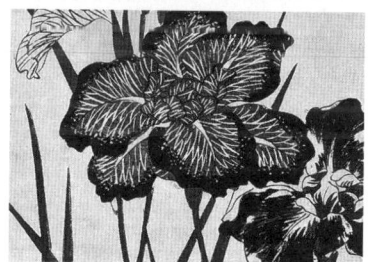

45 | Utagawa Hiroshige II
Irises at Horikiri in Tokyo
series: *Thirty-six Selected Flowers*,
publisher: Tsutaya Kichizō
(Koeido), 1866
oban size, 36.5 x 23.5 cm
Boston, Museum of Fine Arts
(11.37275)

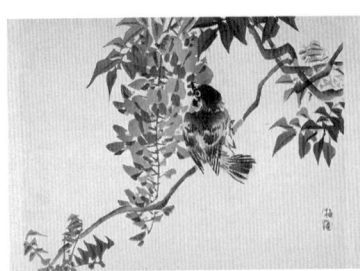

46 | Kōno Bairei
Sparrow on a Wisteria Branch
ca. 1859–95
chuban size, 18 x 23.6 cm
Minneapolis, Minneapolis
Institute of Art (P.77.27.7)

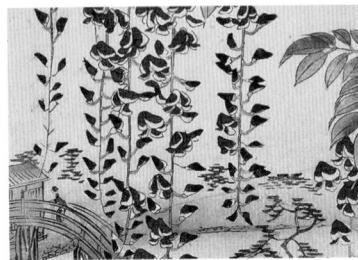

47 | Utagawa Hiroshige II
*Wisteria at Kameido Tenjin Shrine
in the Eastern Capital*
series: *Thirty-six Selected Flowers,*
publisher: Tsutaya Kichizō
(Koeido), 1866
oban size, 36.5 x 23.5 cm
Boston, Museum of Fine Arts
(11.37264)

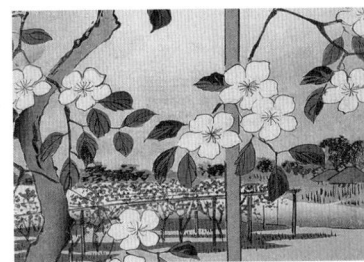

48 | Utagawa Hiroshige II
*Pear Blossoms at Rokuroku
in the Eastern Capital*
series: *Thirty-six Selected Flowers,*
publisher: Tsutaya Kichizō
(Koeido), 1866
oban size, 36.5 x 23.6 cm
Boston, Museum of Fine Arts
(11.37260)

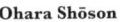

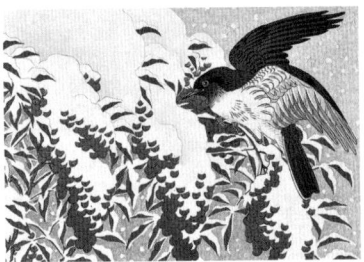

Ohara Shōson
Flycatchers on a Nandina Bush
publisher: Watanabe Shōzaburō,
ca. 1925–36
oban size, 38 x 25.5 cm
Amsterdam, Rijksmuseum
(RP-P-1999-552)
(detail, **see 76**)

49 | Utagawa Hiroshige II
Kirishima Azaleas at Gokoku-ji
Temple in Tokyo
series: *Thirty-six Selected Flowers*,
publisher: Tsutaya Kichizō
(Koeido), 1866
oban size, 36 x 23.5 cm
Boston, Museum of Fine Arts
(01.7335.16)

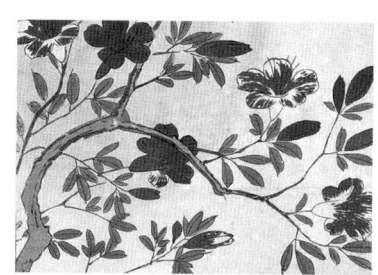

50 | Utagawa Hiroshige II
Peonies at Kitazawa in Tokyo
series: *Thirty-six Selected Flowers*,
publisher: Tsutaya Kichizō
(Koeido), 1866
oban size, 36.5 x 23.7 cm
Boston, Museum of Fine Arts
(11.37281)

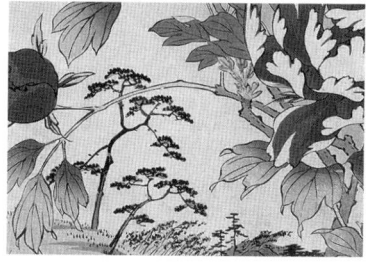

51 | Utagawa Hiroshige II
Primrose at Todahara in Tokyo
series: *Thirty-six Selected Flowers*,
publisher: Tsutaya Kichizō
(Koeido), 1866
oban size, 36.5 x 23.5 cm
Boston, Museum of Fine Arts
(11.37261)

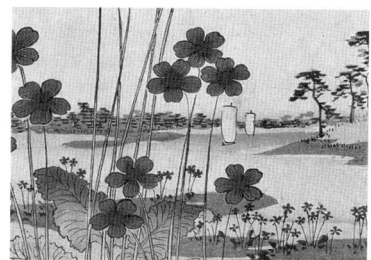

52 | Utagawa Hiroshige II
Camellia at Ueno Shimotera
in the Eastern Capital
series: *Thirty-six Selected Flowers*,
publisher: Tsutaya Kichizō
(Koeido), 1866
oban size, 36.5 x 23.5 cm
Boston, Museum of Fine Arts
(11.37258)

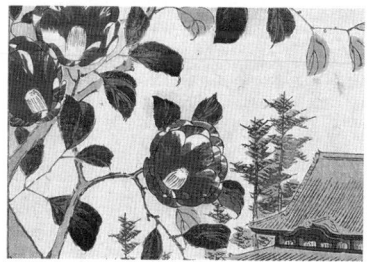

53 | Imao Keinen
Black and White Bird among Pink Roses
series: *Keinen's Bird and Flower Album*,
publisher: Aoki Kozaburo, 1892
20.8 x 27.5 cm
Amsterdam, Rijksmuseum
(RP-P-2004-508D-5)

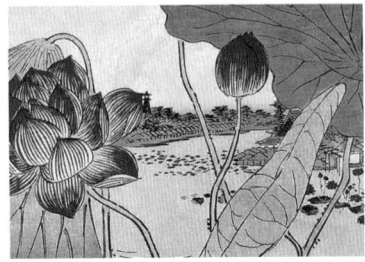

54 | Utagawa Hiroshige II
Lotuses at Shinobazu Pond in Tokyo
series: *Thirty-six Selected Flowers*,
publisher: Tsutaya Kichizō
(Koeido), 1866
oban size, 36.5 x 23.5 cm
Boston, Museum of Fine Arts
(11.37270)

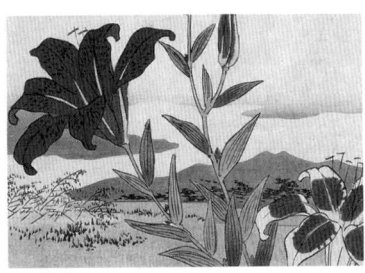

55 | Utagawa Hiroshige II
Lilies at Senju in the Eastern Capital
series: *Thirty-six Selected Flowers*,
publisher: Tsutaya Kichizō
(Koeido), 1866
oban size, 36.5 x 23.5 cm
Boston, Museum of Fine Arts
(11.37280)

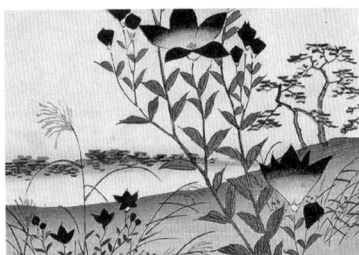

56 | Utagawa Hiroshige II
Bellflowers at Hiroo Plain in Tokyo
series: *Thirty-six Selected Flowers*,
publisher: Tsutaya Kichizō
(Koeido), 1866
oban size, 36.5 x 23.7 cm
Boston, Museum of Fine Arts
(11.37266)

57 | Utagawa Hiroshige II
Morning Glories at Iriya
in the Eastern Capital
series: *Thirty-six Selected Flowers,*
publisher: Tsutaya Kichizō
(Koeido), 1866
oban size, 36 x 23.5 cm
Boston, Museum of Fine Arts
(01.7335.29)

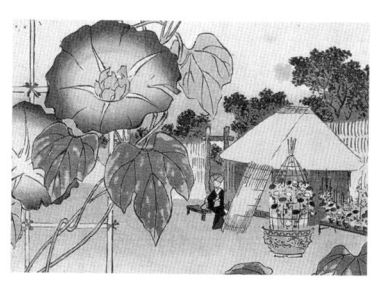

58 | Utagawa Hiroshige II
Hydrangea at the Flower Garden at Asakusa
in the Eastern Capital
series: *Thirty-six Selected Flowers,*
publisher: Tsutaya Kichizō
(Koeido), 1866
oban size, 36 x 23.5 cm
Boston, Museum of Fine Arts
(01.7335.25)

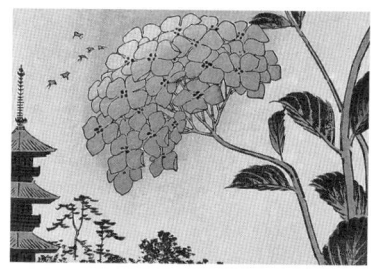

59 | Utagawa Hiroshige II
Cherry Blossoms at Koganei
in the Eastern Capital
series: *Thirty-six Selected Flowers,*
publisher: Tsutaya Kichizō
(Koeido), 1866
oban size, 36 x 23.5 cm
Boston, Museum of Fine Arts
(01.7335.6)

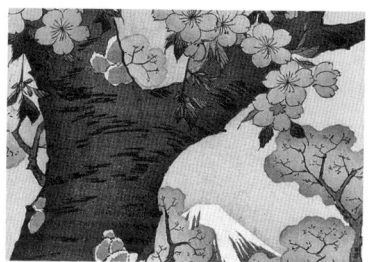

60 | Imao Keinen
Birds and Peonies
series: *Keinen's Bird and Flower Album,*
publisher: Aoki Kozaburo, 1892
20.8 x 27.6 cm
Amsterdam, Rijksmuseum
(RP-P-2004-508B-5)

61 | Utagawa Hiroshige II
Canola Flowers at the Komatsu River in Tokyo
series: *Thirty-six Selected Flowers,*
publisher: Tsutaya Kichizō
(Koeido), 1866
oban size, 36.6 x 23.6 cm
Boston, Museum of Fine Arts
(11.30554)

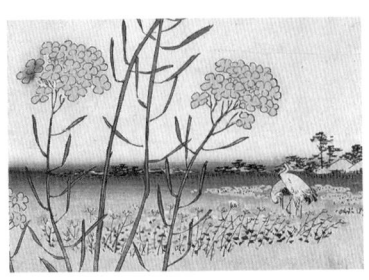

62 | Utagawa Hiroshige II
Hibiscus in the Flower Garden [at Mukojima]
on the Sumida River in the Eastern Capital
series: *Thirty-six Selected Flowers,*
publisher: Tsutaya Kichizō
(Koeido), 1866
oban size, 36.5 x 23.5 cm
Boston, Museum of Fine Arts
(11.37268)

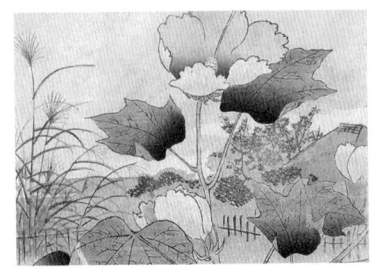

63 | Imao Keinen
Bird and Yellow Flowers
series: *Keinen's Bird and Flower Album,*
publisher: Aoki Kozaburo, 1892
20.9 x 27 cm
Amsterdam, Rijksmuseum
(RP-P-2004-508C-7)

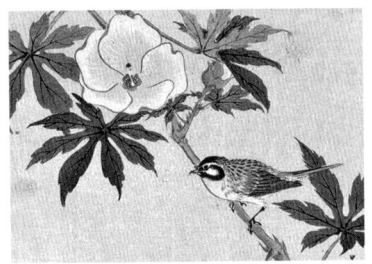

64 | Utagawa Hiroshige III
Morning Glory and Oriental Greenfinch
series: *New Selection of Birds and Flowers,*
1871–73
chuban size, 23.5 x 17.5 cm
Amsterdam, Van Gogh Museum
(n0110-001V1962)

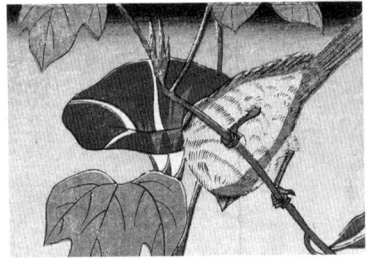

65 | Utagawa Hiroshige III
Peonies and Blue-and-White Flycatcher
series: *New Selection of Birds and Flowers*,
1871–73
chuban size, 23.5 x 17.5 cm
Amsterdam, Van Gogh Museum
(n0110-001V1962)

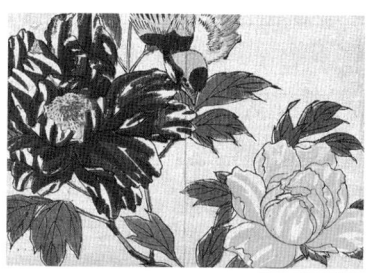

66 | Utagawa Hiroshige II
Hollyhock at Aoizaka in the Eastern Capital
series: *Thirty-six Selected Flowers*,
publisher: Tsutaya Kichizō
(Koeido), 1866
oban size, 36.5 x 23.5 cm
Boston, Museum of Fine Arts
(11.37272)

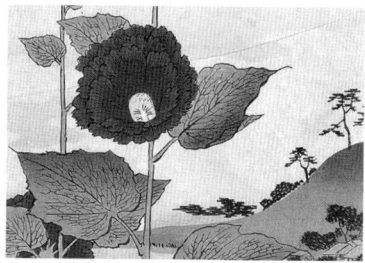

67 | Ohara Shōson
Hollyhocks and Dragonflies
1934
oban size, 36.8 x 24.1 cm
Private Collection

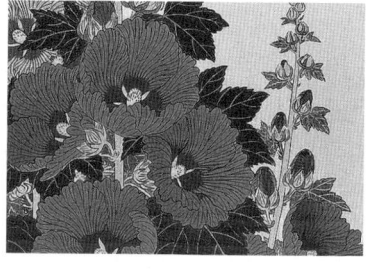

68 | Tanigami Konan
Peonies
1917
wide *oban* size, 56 x 42 cm
Private Collection

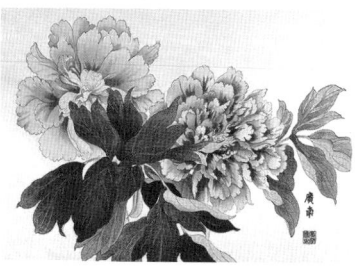

69 | Ohara Shōson
White Lilies
publisher: Kawaguchi, ca. 1930
oban size, 32.5 x 22 cm
Amsterdam, Rijksmuseum
(RP-P-1999-542)

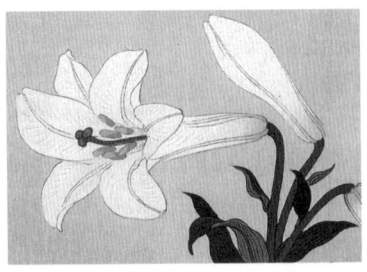

70 | Nishimura Hodo
Tiger Lilies
publisher: Takemura Hideo, ca. 1930
oban size, 36.5 x 24.6 cm
Private Collection

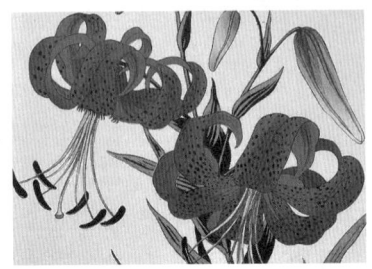

71 | Tanigami Konan
Calla Lily and Lathyrus
1918
Private Collection

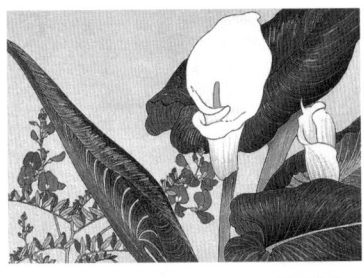

72 | Ohara Shōson
Two Birds and Begonia in Rain
ca. 1936
Private Collection

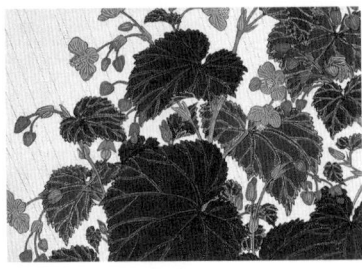

73 | Ohara Shōson
Flycatcher on Rose Mallow Watching Spider
publisher: Watanabe Shōzaburō,
ca. 1932
oban size, 39.2 x 26.1 cm
Private Collection

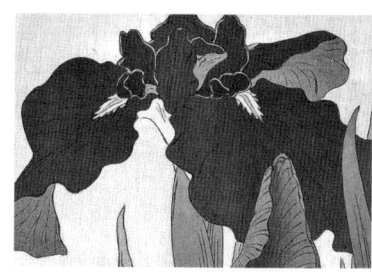

74 | Ohara Shōson
Iris
publisher: Kawaguchi Jirō, ca. 1930
oban size, 32.1 x 21.4 cm
Minneapolis, Minneapolis
Institute of Art (P.75.51.189)

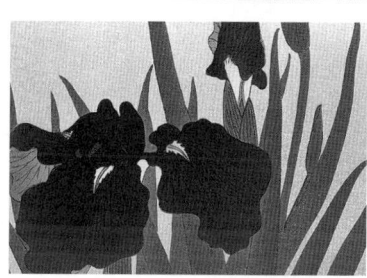

75 | Ohara Shōson
Irises
publisher: Watanabe Shōzaburō,
ca. 1925–36
oban size, 39.5 x 26.5 cm
Amsterdam, Rijksmuseum
(RP-P-1999-553)

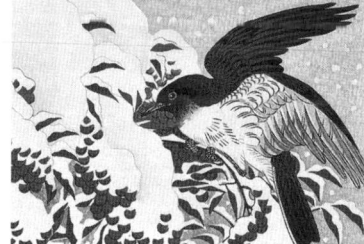

76 | Ohara Shōson
Flycatchers on a Nandina Bush
publisher: Watanabe Shōzaburō,
ca. 1925–36
oban size, 38 x 25.5 cm
Amsterdam, Rijksmuseum
(RP-P-1999-552)

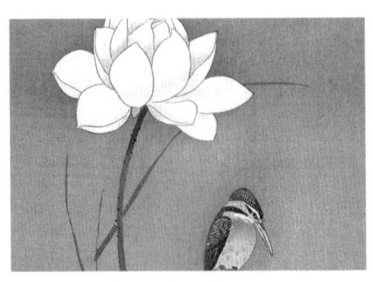

77 | Ohara Shōson
Kingfisher with Lotus Flower
publisher: Nishinomiya Yosaku,
ca. 1900–45
45 x 26.5 cm
Amsterdam, Rijksmuseum
(RP-P-1999-435)

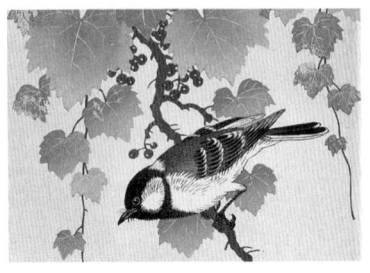

78 | Ohara Shōson
Great Tit on Paulownia Branch
publisher: Watanabe Shōzaburō,
ca. 1925–36
oban size, 38.1 x 25.9 cm
Amsterdam, Rijksmuseum
(RP-P-1999-375)

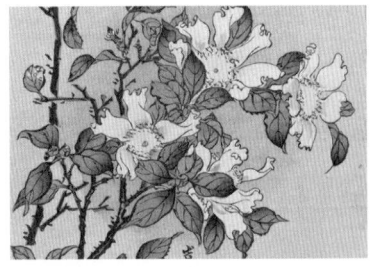

79 | Nakayama Sugakudo
Blue Bird and Pink Flowers
publisher: Tsutaya Kichizō, 1859
oban size, 33.5 x 22 cm
Minneapolis, Minneapolis
Institute of Art (P.75.51.119)

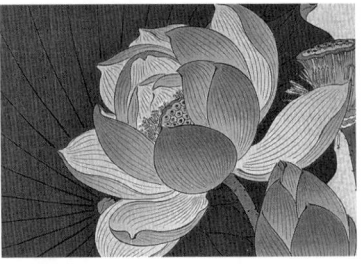

80 | Ohara Shōson
Blooming Lotus Flowers
publisher: Kawaguchi, ca. 1920–30
oban size, 32.2 x 21 cm
Amsterdam, Rijksmuseum
(RP-P-1999-564)

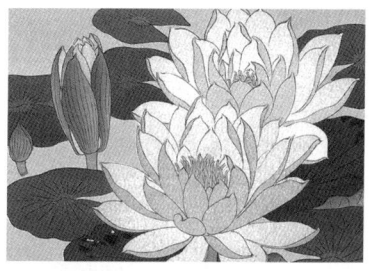

81 | Ohara Shōson
Flowering Water Lily
publisher: Kawaguchi, ca. 1920–30
oban size, 37.7 x 24.1 cm
Amsterdam, Rijksmuseum
(RP-P-1999-381)

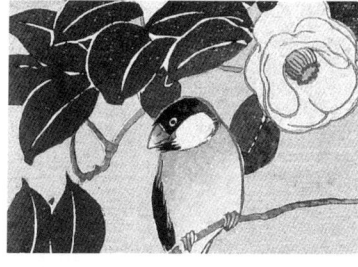

82 | Itō Sōzan
Bird and Camellia
ca. 1930
Private Collection

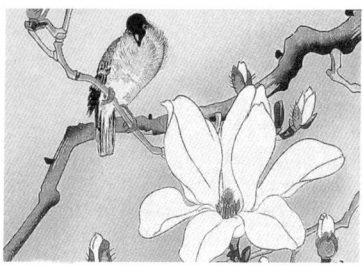

83 | Watanabe Seitei
Bird on Magnolia
Private Collection

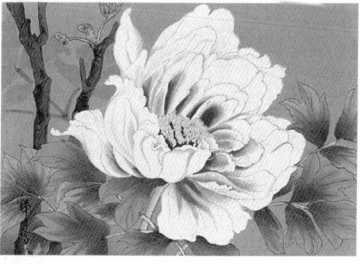

84 | Zuigetsu Ikeda
Pink Camellia
publisher: Unsodo, ca. 1950
oban size, 38.7 x 28.5 cm
Private Collection

Photo Credits

Amsterdam, Rijksmuseum: pp. 8–9; figs. 19, 44, 53, 60, 63, 69, 75, 76, 77, 78, 80, 81

Amsterdam, Van Gogh Museum: figs. 64, 65

Boston, Museum of Fine Arts: pp. 11, 14–15, 16; figs. 1, 5, 7, 14, 15, 16, 18, 20, 28, 29, 30, 31, 35, 45, 47, 48, 49, 50, 51, 52, 54, 55, 56, 57, 58, 59, 61, 62, 66

Chicago, The Art Institute of Chicago: pp. 4, 19

Minneapolis, Minneapolis Institute of Art: figs. 6, 17, 27, 32, 46, 74, 79

New York, The Metropolitan Museum of Art: pp. 12–13, 20; figs. 2, 3, 4, 8, 9, 10, 11, 12, 13, 23, 24, 25, 26, 33, 34, 36, 37, 38, 39, 40, 41, 42, 43

Private Collections: figs. 22, 67, 68, 70, 71, 72, 73, 82, 83, 84

Washington, DC, National Museum of Asian Art: fig. 21

Washington, DC, Smithsonian Libraries: p. 17

Slipcase: Ohara Shōson, *Iris*, publisher: Kawaguchi Jirō, ca. 1930, Minneapolis, Minneapolis Institute of Art

The author would like to thank the entire team at Éditions Hazan: Anne-Isabelle Vanier, Jérôme Gille, and Marie-Hélène Durand de Corbiac for their trust and enthusiasm, Anne Chapoutot for her careful proofreading, as well as Frédéric Wronski.

For Éditions Hazan

Editorial Director
Jérôme Gille

Editorial Supervisor
Anne-Isabelle Vannier

Graphic Research
Amélie Balcou

Production
Claire Hostalier and Pierre Hamard

Photoengraving
Reproscan, Orio al Serio, Italy